MW01002842

HOW TO START A SIX FIGURE PUBLISHING COMPANY

A Guide for Ambitious Female Entrepreneurs Who Are Ready to Transform a Formerly Male-Dominated Industry

ADRIANA MONIQUE ALVAREZ

PUBLISHING

in self talk

Contents

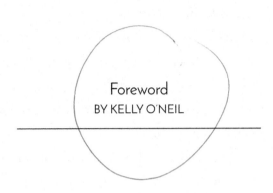

Foreword

BY KELLY O'NEIL

For generations the traditional publishing industry has predominantly been a white, male driven industry. In its archaic module, it can take years to bring brilliance to market and is subject to the different publishing houses to determine if the content will sell. Not if it is brilliant. Not if it is groundbreaking or thought provoking. But if it will sell.

On the flip side of the coin, quick-turn fast food type self-publishing houses popped up right and left allowing any human with extra time on their hands and something to say the opportunity to get instant gratification of throwing a book out in to market. This, in itself, has created a separate issue. According to the latest ProQuest Bowker Report (October 15, 2019), nearly 1.7 million books were self-published in the U.S. in 2018, which is an incredible 264% increase in just five years.

The publishing industry is in need of a disruption and Adriana is leading the way.

For the last twenty years, I've been consulting entrepreneurs on how to strategically disrupt markets, become known as the go-to authorities in the markets and rapidly accelerate their business growth by working smart, not hard.

I reach hundreds of thousands of entrepreneurs worldwide through media, speaking and social networking each year. I blessed to be a Forbes and Entrepreneur contributing author and have been featured in Wall Street Journal, Fortune, NBC, and ABC, Business Journal and many others.

I am blessed to have shared the stage with industry legends including Tim Ferris, Jack Canfield, Brian Tracey, Bob Proctor, John Assaraf, Mark Victor Hansen, Les Brown, Tony Hsieh, and Lisa Nichols among other brilliant influencers.

I've been around the block. I've seen the entrepreneurial industry grow and change. I've watched the leaders who have broken through the fray and the wanna-be "me too" clan who struggles to break through.

I met Adriana through my Marketing to Millionaires Business Acceleration program. From the moment she joined, she stood out. She gets it.

I've watched as she adopted our business acceleration model to skyrocket her business in less than 60 days, while she is disrupting the status quo in publishing and leading the way to reshape an entire industry. She has created a business model that teaches women how to create highly profitable publishing houses by focusing on those who are brilliant change makers, influencers, and committed to success.

This book will guide you through Adriana's alternative approach to break into a notoriously intimidating industry and get into cash flow fast.

There is an infinite amount of wealth in the world RIGHT NOW. And money puts you in a place of choice and provides you with the opportunity to create real impact and influence. That is where the change really occurs.

Through this book, you have the choice to lean in and create a new stream of income from what most people already know they want, an opportunity for their story to be heard.

Fortune favors the bold. It's time for you to leap.

Introduction
WHERE I STAND

I have a deep appreciation for men — I have the best father ever, I am married to the best man on the planet, and am the mother of two strong little boys.

When I was recently asked if I would change my model and branding to include men, I had to pause and ask myself, why do I only serve women?

Truth be told, I only had two female clients for the first seven years of business; men were our clientele.

This all changed when I had two babies in twelve months. The men moved on and the women moved in. This was not a decision on my part, it just happened.

No one knows what it means to be a woman and mother in business like another woman and mother. I did calls holding babies; I ran meetings with little ones at my feet, and now if everyone doesn't meet my son Grant during a call, it's a miracle.

I didn't apologize for it—I still don't. In fact, I said, this is what it looks like and it doesn't make us any less qualified.

My children helped me find my fire and my deep internal roar. They showed me where I was wasting time and thinking small.

So after looking inside my heart, I realized I am passionate about creating 10,000 female-owned publishing houses by 2027 because most of the ones that exist don't celebrate and honor women and mothers in leadership roles.

They see children and pregnancy as a disability. Women chose me and now it's easy for me to choose them.

I am honored to train and support women.

I am blessed to work around my children.

And when it's all said and done, I want mothers to remember that I understood them and championed their dreams.

The next generation is watching, and backing mothers is no longer special; it's non-negotiable.

How I Live and Work

Nina visits me at 3 am almost every day. She is the Ascended Master who has taken me on in this life. She is also the soul I hosted in my womb for 38 weeks, and when I asked her why that was necessary she said, "So you would know how real the other side is." In that moment, I stopped beating myself up, I stopped questioning, I really got it.

What do we do in the early morning, you might wonder.

Her presence is so powerful and it leads to me calling back all my power. I gather all the parts of myself and I acknowledge the God-ness that is me.

From this space, I connect to my other key Guides, Iris, Grandma, and Mother Mary, and then to my Angels and Ancestors that are with me on this property. To the animals, trees, flowers, grass, soil and sky.

Then I connect to Derek's soul and send him love for being here with me, for supporting the evolution of my soul, and for assisting me in completing my soul's mission. I do the same with the boys and my parents.

And then I send my love and attention out to the Universe.

I connect to my Soul family and to every soul I came here to co-create with in any capacity. I remind myself and all beings of how we agreed to support each other in this life.

I commit to them that I will shine my light and use my voice and connect energetically every day so we can easily find one another and remember who we are here to be. I send them courage and love as I invite them to step closer.

And then I direct all my attention to my heart and body. I breathe in the love and support of the Universe. I acknowledge my higher self—the one that has perspective and wisdom beyond the here and now.

I give my Unseen team permission to assist me in my day. I feel all the good that is present in my body, my family, my life. I sense all the good in the world and I see it multiply. I lay in silence, knowing all is well. Life supports me. I am present. I am ready for this beautiful day. I am open to receiving everything the Universe has for me.

However this book has landed in your hands, it is not by coincidence.

I could have never imagined I would own a publishing company, much less be showing women from around the world how to start their own.

I was sitting in a moment of utter frustration, feeling constrained and as if someone had clipped my wings. I sat in my grandma's chair and asked her and Nina to help me.

What can I do to be BIGGER than what's happening outside of me? And like the first time my angel baby Nina spoke to me, it was a lightning bolt moment.

So loud.

So clear.

So real.

It coursed through my body and I knew beyond a shadow of a doubt, this was it!

I am one person, but if hundreds of women — thousands of women create — opportunities through books, VOICES WILL BE HEARD.

Now it's all I think about. I eat, drink, and breathe this. Who is the next woman being called to start a publishing house? Every morning I ask for them to raise their hand and act. I've been given the structure, the support team, and the ideas to make it as big as they can imagine it.

We can't afford to ask:

Why me?

Am I qualified enough?

Am I good enough?

What if?

It's time we say I AM HERE.

Ready, willing, and able.

Before I go into why female-owned publishing houses matter or how to jump into this industry, let me start with what we stand for at AMA Publishing.

We Believe in Success by Association

Who we associate with matters. Who we create alliances with makes the difference. When you align with us, you align with success, and the community you gain access to will offer collaborations of the highest level—networking with other leading women is not only allowed, but also encouraged in our circle.

We Believe in Being the Right Person

Many programs focus on doing the right things at the right time. However, we believe in being the right person first. Taking action is non-negotiable and what matters most is who we are while taking that action. We encourage our students to do the work that no one sees, connecting to the highest part of themselves and showing up as the most fully expressed women they can be. No one is really buying what we sell; they are buying into our presence, our energy, and our values. Figuring this out first will make everything else feel effortless.

We Believe in Leading the Way

Being congruent with what we teach, who we are, and what we do is key. We continuously provide opportunities for our students to practice using their voice, being visible, and expanding their reach. We know that leading means going first and never asking our clients to do more than we are willing to do. Becoming a better leader day by day is our calling, duty, and honor.

We Believe in Being Bold

Walking on eggshells and hiding in the back row is not who we are. We believe in turning it up so that the world knows with absolute certainty who we are and what we are here to do. Being a mousy, humble, doormat of a woman is not what we are here to perpetuate. There is no such thing as being too much in our world. We long to link arms with women who are loud and proud of what they are passionate about.

We Believe in Leaving a Legacy

What our children and grandchildren receive as a result of our efforts is valuable to us. We are here to leave not only a financial blessing but a literary footprint for those who come after us. Our children's children will know what we did with this precious life and it will empower them to live out their soul's calling to the fullest extent.

You might be wondering what kind of women start their own publishing company.

The fun part is that our clients are incredibly diverse and from around the world. The list includes birth and parenting experts, former corporate professionals who have worked with Fortune 500 companies, spiritual leaders, healers and shamans, holistic health coaches, practitioners, yoga instructors, retreat facilitators, business consultants, book coaches, editors and ghost-writers, finance professionals, VA and web development agency owners, and ministers to name a few.

Why these women start their publishing company is also varied but amplifying voices is one of their core values. They also desire to elevate their business. For example, being a business coach is one thing, adding a publishing division that creates opportunities to become a bestselling author is another. Our students think bigger and know what their audiences desire and are ready to step up and provide it.

Why they choose to go through our certification process is simple: they want to access a structured, proven system and the community that comes along with it.

Why Female-Owned Publishing
Houses Matter

*I*t has been said that publishing is a gentleman's career. What I learned in my research is that while it was common for women to have supporting roles in publishing, they were restricted from becoming professional publishers through custom and law in America until the late 19th century. Similar trends occurred in the UK and Canada; women typically assumed control of publishing only after the death of their husband or a male relative.

Elizabeth Timothy is often recognized as the first female newspaper publisher in America. She worked in partnership with Benjamin Franklin to publish the *South Carolina Gazette* in the 1730s and 1740s (after the death of her husband, who was Franklin's original partner). As was typical of the time, the *Gazette* was not published under her name, but rather her son's—who was a mere teenager at the time —but who legally took over his father's business.

Throughout the 19th century, the rise of large publishing houses and the middle class meant that more and more women sought out careers for themselves in publishing. Yet publishing maintained a reputation of being a "gentleman's profession." The business was still built around an idea of who an editor knew, the "old boy's networks" that made connections between authors, agents, and publishers.

Books were acquired and business collaborations happened informally with the elite connections that men had cultivated through their families, college connections, or social circles. Most women at publishing houses often held lower-paying, clerical positions.

According to a 1916 career guide for girls, "editors, the reporters, and the men who rewrite stories must be able to work under the pressure in a way that is beyond the power of most women."

Today, women make up the majority of those employed in publishing, but still tend to dominate in lower-level positions, and typically earn less than their male counterparts.

I am here to change this.

When I added publishing to my business, I instinctively knew the power of my work multiplied.

Having witnessed what happens when women are given a safe space to fully communicate and express even one story, I knew I wanted to make this an integral part of my work.

The writing process is transformational. It is as if women access new parts of themselves when they are given the space to share a story that is deeply personal, powerful, and raw.

Sharing stories breaks the chains of silence that hold women in a bubble of powerlessness and being in a community with others who are doing the same generates courage that so many have longed to tap into.

The personal growth is tremendous and I do not want to omit the professional growth that is possible. Imagine what is possible when there are 20 or more women unified through the theme of the book. Having access to twenty more networks, communities, social media circles, and email lists for starters.

When my clients shared their stories far and wide through the books I produced, I witnessed them receive opportunities to be featured in the media and invitations to be on podcasts and summits.

Right before my eyes, I saw the way they promoted their service and improved and held a passion that didn't exist before.

They raised their prices and sold out programs because they sensed their audience change the way they perceived them, so they responded accordingly.

I want to make it very clear: I teach my students how to create successful female-owned publishing houses but it doesn't only benefit them; their clients are richer for participating.

I'll share my experiences as we go along but I truly saw the power of multi-author books when I was invited to share my story in one. I did it as a favor because I respected the person producing it, but I honestly didn't believe it would do much for my business.

I wrote my chapter in three days, turned it in, and got back to my life and business.

A few weeks later, I was informed about the launch date and encouraged to create an offer to promote in conjunction with the release of the book. I quickly put together a simple training on how to make $100k from a Facebook group. Within 14 days of the launch, 68 people purchased my program. A month later, I put out an up-sell and 27 people purchased that. I then introduced my high end package and three said yes to that. In less than six months, I had received over $82k that was directly related to the book launch.

Combine that with the fact that almost every client I had worked with for the previous ten years had the desire to write a book, but most never got around to it. They didn't know who they could trust and the entire process felt overwhelming.

That is when AMA Publishing was born.

Through trial and error I mapped out the process you will learn in this book and that I teach every woman who comes through our program. I already made all the mistakes so you don't have to.

I produced six international bestselling multi-author books in addition to working with amazing solo authors. I had a full affiliate team and things were humming along, but I knew I could not produce enough books to share the stories that were ready to be told.

I am one person.

The day I heard, "certify women to start their own publishing house and multiply the reach," I could feel every cell in my being light up and I knew this was my next step. I reached out to key clients and put the word out on social media. A handful of women accepted to participate and became the first students in the AMA Publishing Certification Program.

They had very different backgrounds and areas of expertise, but the thing they had in common is they created books, sold them out, and launched. Their clients had the same experience my clients did—they dramatically increased their income and influence.

It worked!

Now we are duplicating the results over and over again with women just like you. The graduates are on track to have six-figure and even multiple six-figure incomes in their first year. Some are even landing six-figure contracts.

There is no limit to what we can create through this business model and mission.

The best part is the graduates are now becoming trainers. After women successfully produce at least two bestsellers and make $50k or more in their publishing company, they can apply to the AMA Publishing Certification Program 2.0 where they learn how to reach seven figures in their publishing company and become teachers in the 1.0 program.

Our students get to learn from a variety of voices, backgrounds, and expertise, which is gold.

Not only that, we have a team of pros at producing books, so our students never have to worry about creating cover designs, editing chapters, formatting books, or getting bogged down with the Amazon process.

I am changing the pattern of women not being fully supported for success.

Every single student is equipped with the necessary resources to create a high-income, high-impact publishing house.

With every female-owned publishing house, we are breaking the silence and reminding women there is power in their voice. We are creating platforms and mediums for their voices to be heard on global platforms. The right to tell a story, to share a truth, and to be heard is a form of wealth.

Female-owned publishing houses create opportunities for those who have powerful stories to share.

Silence is not golden and the time for women to be seen and heard is now.

Are you the kind of woman that wants to be part of this revolution?

ADRIANA MONIQUE ALVAREZ

I created a 37 minute masterclass on the 3 most important steps to starting, click here to watch it:

www.adrianamoniquealvarez.com/how-to-start-your-own-publishing-company

2

How to Position Yourself in the Marketplace

I know what is going through your mind. You are excited by the thought of creating this kind of business, but you have no idea where to start and you are not certain you have the skill set necessary to be successful. This is completely normal!

The good news is that most of my clients have zero experience in publishing when they join my certification program, but they had the passion and felt the call to get started.

If you are willing to be the student, learn, experiment, and have fun along the way, not only will you grow, you will create a highly profitable publishing company that serves on many levels.

The necessary first step is to remember this isn't about you.

It isn't about whether or not you have a degree, experience, success, or failures; this is about understanding that most people in the world have an untold story inside of them and they are looking for the opportunity to change that.

If you wish to experience the most success in the shortest amount of time, shift the focus off yourself and your perceived shortcomings to the desires of your prospective clients.

Here are a few questions to ask yourself as you begin this process:

Who would be fun and interesting to have in my books?

Where are they in their business and career?

What is their annual income?

Once again, I am here to remind you that you are the CEO and you get to choose everything; the key is to be intentional about each step.

What kinds of people do you work best with? For example, I am a fast-paced person with a Human Design of a Manifesting Generator so it is only natural that I prefer to work with people who also work fast. I have always been like this and I resented every teacher that paired me with the slower student on group projects.

For this reason, I do not punish those who work

quickly in my certification program. Every person can go at the pace that works for them and those fast movers and overachievers never have to wait for anyone in my programs.

What kind of people do you find interesting? Whose stories would you like to highlight?

As you can tell, I am a big fan of women in business and those who build empires with kids at their feet are my heroes. I created titles and books that spoke right to this kind of woman because I wanted to create space for women to share their wisdom and encourage those coming behind them.

When it comes to looking at where your contributors are in their career or business, I highly recommend positioning yourself right in front of those who are at least three years in and making at least $100k a year.

When people are making less in their business, most of their focus is on staying afloat and paying bills. These people tend to invest less often in themselves simply because they do not have the necessary budget.

When people are making six figures or more in their career or business, most of their focus is on growth and expansion.

There are always going to be exceptions to this

rule. For example, there might be women who are new to business and not quite in cash flow but have a healthy savings account or a spouse who supports them as they grow their business.

Some are ambitious and resourceful and always find a way to move forward.

Trust me when I say everything falls into place when you learn how to present your books in a clear, distinctive, and desirable way so your prospective contributors see themselves as being a good fit for your projects.

It might sound ridiculous, but no one initially cares about who you are or what your publishing house's name is, or if your latest photos are as pretty as Sally Sue's.

Your audience and the audiences that you have access to through social media only care about the books you produce.

If the title and theme speak to them, they will self-select and there will be no need for you to explain and convince them that you are worthy of their trust. Now that is not to say, that I won't teach you how to create trust many times over through this process, but it is not what will grab them immediately.

You must be absolutely clear on the types of books you wish to create, the topics and stories you want to represent, and the type of authors you prefer to work with.

As the CEO of your publishing company, you get to decide all of this.

Since you get to choose, you might as well choose the best, right? Why not work with the best clients on the planet? That means considering what you are passionate about and what they could contribute a story to, and are more than happy to pay your fees.

You could be thinking your current audience or past clients are not a good fit for this particular enterprise.

That is ok!

In a world of eight billion people, one billion of which are on Facebook alone, don't you think that 25 or 100 of them are perfect for you and your books?

One of the practices I have developed for myself over the years is telling myself the truth every single day. I say things like:

People want to work with me.

People love connecting with me.

There are people right now looking for exactly what I provide.

My audience loves reading my content.

The best people are moving toward me.

When I take action, it works.

When I am present with my life, I am in flow.

My clients love paying me for what I provide.

I love receiving money.

If this is also how you speak to yourself, great! If it isn't, you can change this today. I still remember when I decided to become my biggest fan and cheerleader.

Like many of my clients, I was born an over-achiever. I was a straight-A student with perfect attendance, a leader, and a president-of-it-all kind of person. The problem was that I was incredibly hard on myself. I had nearly impossible standards and the mean girl was me and she was always telling me off.

I could never be good enough, which also led to comparing myself to everyone and feeling awful.

Everyone was better, more capable, prettier, more popular, and I was left trying harder.

Early on in my business, I realized this wasn't going to work out well for me if I continued. I had years of practice so I knew I had to change my daily habits if I was going to turn this around. Every morning, as soon as I woke up, I wrote out what was now true about me. Then I said them out loud all day long. When I was driving, running errands, when I was in the shower, and maybe most importantly when I was with other people.

I chose to fully love and accept myself exactly the way I was.

I am dedicated to a lifelong path of improvement and growth, but I no longer let that be a reason to suspend self-acceptance.

I also changed my nightly ritual of rehashing everything that didn't go quite the way I planned, the things I was disappointed with, and all the ways I had been less than perfect. Instead, I focused my attention right before falling asleep on all the sweetest moments of my day.

My husband and I also decided that we would celebrate our week, wins, and accomplishments every Friday. This combination contributed to me becoming a woman who celebrates and champions herself.

Interestingly enough, I found that the best women want to be around me because who doesn't want to be around a woman who loves and values herself? Being in that energy is refreshing for my clients and it allows them to do the same.

I said all this to say if you go through this book thinking, "who am I to do this," you will miss out on the many gifts available to you now.

So, will you promise me that you will say, "why not me and accept that you are capable of changing the world through the powerful work you do?"

Be sure to download my YOU ARE THE BEST digital file in the private Facebook group once you sign up for my free masterclass:

www.adrianamoniquealvarez.com/how-to-start-your-own-publishing-company

All right, now let's look at how to create the concept for your first multi-author book.

3

How to Get Started

There are two main types of books that boutique publishing houses create:

1. Solo author books
2. Multi-author books

Now you might be wondering why I don't lead with solo author books and it's because if you are new to publishing and do not have testimonials or case studies, it can be more difficult to land these clients.

On the other hand, if you produce a multi-author book, you'll find that a handful of your contributors will be ready to write their solo books and will already have a relationship with you, making you an obvious choice for them.

The other thing is that solo books are daunting for the average person, especially if they are also running a business.

Most people who desire to write a book haven't finished because they:

- Believe they do not have the time.
- Lack clear guidance and support.
- Do not have $10k to invest in the project.

Now we know that everyone has 24 hours in a day but some make much better use of their time than others.

When I wrote my first solo book, I was traveling full time and living in Mexico. My boys were 1 and 2 respectively and I was running a business. I knew if I devoted some time to my book each day, I could get it done, but I had to be smart about it. I decided to ask my husband to nap the boys each day, and that was when I packed up my laptop and went to my favorite coffee shop to write. I sat there for two hours or until I had written three thousand words and then I went back home to make meals, get on client calls, or whatever needed my attention.

Within three months, I had written my book and got it ready for Amazon.

I had recently moved my business online after being local for the first seven years. I traded my BNI membership for going live on Facebook every day and I was on a mission to show the online world that I had experience and could be trusted.

I went live and asked 50 women to purchase the book when it was released and share it with their community. My plan worked and the book led to a sold out Mastermind. I was invited on many podcasts and then I decided to start pitching to publications. Within that year, I wrote for or was featured on Forbes, Huffington Post, International Living, Elephant Journal, and Addicted2Success.

Taking the time to write that book completely changed the trajectory of my business.

The truth is most people are reluctant to give up spending time on the internet to write their books. If they do not believe they have the time, larger obstacles will appear which they simply won't even try to overcome.

This is why I recommend starting with a multi-author book.

So, what is a multi-author book and how can you create one?

A multi-author book is a compilation of chapters that 20 or more authors contribute to within a specific theme. Each chapter allows the contributor to bond with the reader. Authors are taught how to write their chapter—typically 3000 words long—and bio to encourage readers to follow them on social media, join their group, or access their offers.

The participation fee can vary, but for the strategies, I stress to my student to charge no less than US$1000, paid in full by the contributors.

Multi-author books make it possible for your clients to become published authors for a fraction of the price of a solo book—not to mention the other benefits such as networking and collaboration partners.

Now let's look at who the ideal participants in a multi-author book are: a wide range, including online coaches, consultants, course creators, corporate leaders, and network marketers. Anyone who wants more visibility for their brand, business, and career path is a great fit. Last but not least, entrepreneurs who would like to instantly elevate their authority and credibility are good leads.

Bottom line: if you market to those who wish to see a return on their investment, you are golden.

If you are reading this and you feel intimidated to

work with these kinds of people, let me remind you: they put their pants on one leg at a time just like you do.

No, seriously, anytime I am afraid to go after highly successful, capable, influential clients, I pause because something is going on inside of me that is creating drag and friction. There is a belief or thought that is creating the emotion and it is not pointing me in the best direction.

One of the mantras I created for myself years ago was, "I work with the best people on earth," and guess what? It became a self-fulfilling prophecy. This is the first step of an epic journey and you want to make sure you begin on the right foot.

Here is a fact: most people who start something new—anything; a business, a workout routine, a relationship—have feelings of doubt.

I have found the absolute best way to work through these feelings before they lead to isolation and self-sabotage is to commit to radical transparency and accountability.

When you hear the soundtrack of *I Don't Think I Can Do This* playing on repeat, break the silence and tell someone.

Separate feelings from facts

"I feel like no one likes me" and "my latest post on social media didn't get any comments," are two very different things.

Accentuate the positive

Instead of trying to be someone you aren't, lean into your natural abilities and strengths.

Develop a healthy response to failure and mistakes

You are human and that is a beautiful thing. The sooner you stop beating yourself for this, the better you and everyone around you will be.

Write a new story

The minute you become aware of the mean girl inside your head, say the words, *cancel* and *delete*. Choose to write a new script and say it often.

Visualize how you want it to be

Pausing for a few minutes a day to sit with your eyes closed and seeing how you want your audience to respond to you, or what you want your business to feel like is a powerful exercise. Allow yourself to bring in emotions and details, make it real in your mind and it will show up in your world.

Now let's make this real. Pop into the private Facebook group and share what you will tell yourself every day as you embark on this new adventure by signing up for my free masterclass here:

www.adrianamoniquealvarez.com/how-to-start-your-own-publishing-company

4

The Single Best Way to Sell Out
Your Book in 30 Days or Less

*a*s I mentioned earlier, you get to decide how many contributors you accept in each of your multi-author books. For the strategies, I teach it is important to sell at least 20 spots, but there is no limit.

The books that sell out the fastest are the ones that have the most impactful theme.

It is tempting to think that you will easily get many contributors if you select a broad theme that will appeal to many people but the truth is actually the opposite.

Choosing a theme that inspires a very niche title is non-negotiable if you want to sell out fast. Some of my clients have sold books out in two or three weeks and every single time they had a polarizing title.

These are the three things I keep in mind when selecting a theme.

1. I am passionate about it.

It is best when the theme of your book is something you are passionate about because you will talk about your book all the time. Before and after you sell it out, it will be the topic of many conversations over months. Make sure you love it and that it fires you up.

2. It is easy for others to see themselves in it.

It is best when the theme of your book is something other people can relate to and can see themselves participating in. If it is vague, people will think it is a nice idea, but they will not be able to see themselves in the project. Self-selection is incredibly important for easy sales.

3. It excludes most of the population.

Your books, even if they had 100 contributors each, are highly exclusive experiences. Most of the population will not be right for them and this is a good thing. Mass appeal is never what we are after. Keep your books unique and super focused on a small group of individuals. If your authors feel as if they are in a highly exclusive experience, you are on the right track.

When people read your title in a social media post or email, you want them to immediately think, *oh my god this is me! I have something to say about this and I must be part of this project. My story needs to be in this book and I cannot let this opportunity pass me by!*

This is key when it comes to getting contributors who are a good fit, can easily invest in themselves, and pay quickly.

We do not believe in putting anyone in a neck hold; we believe in creating projects that people have no desire to stall, delay, or procrastinate on.

The energy your book carries comes from two main places: your energy and the title. Remember every word matters.

Before we attempt to create a title and subtitle, though, I want you to create a theme or decide on a topic first.

What kind of stories do I want to feature in my first book?

Ask yourself this question in the early part of the

day or right before you go to sleep and then write down what comes to mind. Keep in mind, it might not show up right away, but if you have asked the question, it will also show up—sometimes when you're in the shower or driving, or in quiet meditation.

Another great question you can ask yourself is, "how do I want people to feel when they read these stories?"

Remember this: the books your publishing house will create will most likely be inspired by themes that you could write about.

There is an art to creating great book titles and I cannot emphasize enough the need to have at least ten to choose from before selecting your final title.

Your title needs to hit at least most of these marks:

1. Be punchy - When a title has at least one or two words that grab the reader's attention, it is a winner.
2. Be unique - Picking titles that include commonly used topics and words like leadership and business—it is necessary to make them unique.
3. Be easy to say - Select a title that won't be

difficult for you, your contributors, and the audience to pronounce.

Here are a few examples of titles that my clients have created, successfully sold out, and launched on Amazon:

Baby Got VBAC: An inspiring Collection of Wisdom for Better Births After a Cesarean
(Colleen Reagan Noon)

Leading Through the Pandemic: Unconventional Wisdom from Heartfelt Leaders
(Kayleigh O'Keefe)

Wild Woman Rising: Brave Women Who Have Carved Their Own Path
(Tarsh Ashwin)

Here are the titles of the books I produced:

Trailblazers: 27 Female Leaders Share How They Use Their Gifts To Guide Others

Leaders: Women Who Change The World Through Their Business

Empire Moms: Women Who Built Their Business For, Around, and With Their Children

Phoenix: Inspiring Stories of Women Who Have Overcome Challenges & Risen To Find Hope & Purpose

Awakening: Meet the Women Birthing a New Earth

Visionary: The Future Belongs To Those Who Can See In The Dark

Now it's your turn to create titles and subtitles. It takes patience to land on a great title. I get a blank piece of paper and write down the themes I am interested in and then I add titles or bold keywords as they come to me.

Here are a few prompts that will put you on the right path:

1. Does my title make people want to read the subtitle?
2. Does my subtitle further define my title?
3. Does my title capture the essence of my book?
4. Does my title emotionally connect?
5. Does my title tell the reader what they will learn in my book?

After you have at least ten titles, look at the individual words and see if they are the most descriptive, powerful words you can use. Eliminate all unnecessary words and keep the boldest ones.

I like to pick my three favorites and then ask myself, "who would have a story to share in this book? What is their business or career? What are they passionate about? How can this book help them expand their influence?"

It is also a good idea to search your favorites titles online and see if there are books with the same title and subtitle.

A great next step is to test them out on social media. Your audience will quickly reflect if they can see themselves in the title or if it creates confusion.

Once you have tested it out, it is time to pick the one and list at least ten professions or types of business owners that would be a good fit in the book. Once these have been decided, it's time to start talking.

If you would like to pop your top three titles in the private Facebook group, it is absolutely a safe space for you to get helpful feedback. You can join the group once you've signed up for my free masterclass here:

www.adrianamoniquealvarez.com/how-to-start-your-own-publishing-company

5

Where to Find Contributors for
Your Books

*I*f starting a publishing house excites you, you will probably find ideas for books coming easily to you.

If you like the idea of creating opportunities for others to use their voice, you will probably find this business to be very fulfilling.

What you may not feel confident about is selling spots in your books.

And that's ok.

Most of the women I work with do not see themselves as natural salespeople. In fact, they might have a history that tells them they aren't any good at it.

I encourage you to let the past be the past. It happened, it is real, and it is not your future unless you choose it to be.

There are many ways to fill your books, but strategies are only as effective as the person behind them. What does that mean? If you aren't feeling good and if you don't believe in yourself, people will not have any desire to be in your books, even if they cannot pinpoint why.

So let's start with you because you aren't really selling spots in a book; you are selling access to your energy, belief, and vision.

Pause and take a deep breath and as you let it all out, imagine yourself one day, one month, and one year from now.

What will be different about you?

What will be different about your situation?

What will be different about your business?

How will you feel differently about yourself and the work you are here to do?

What if sales meant nothing more than you being as *you* as you can be?

What if sales meant you were completely connected to yourself, your heart, your desires, and the big vision you have for your publishing house?

What if sales meant simply having conversations with people about the fire burning in your soul?

What if sales meant being in a space where the best people can effortlessly see and hear you?

Now picture yourself interacting with the world around you from this new perspective.

Does this feel better?

As I share a handful of strategies (I teach many more in my certification program) I invite you to approach them with childlike curiosity. Experiment with them and do not expect to perfect the practice the first time you try it. Mastery comes over time, with focused intention, and repetition.

Here are a few tips to keep in mind as you start talking about your book projects:

MEANING

If you give every 'yes' or 'no' meaning, it will become exhausting. If a post gets crickets instead of 300 likes and you assign meaning to it, you might not post again.

Instead of every single thing you do or your audience does having meaning, see if you can ask yourself these questions instead and stay loose in the process:

1. What am I learning about myself
   right now?
2. What lesson can I take from this?
3. How can things turn out differently next
   time if I keep going?
4. In the grand scheme of things, how much
   does this matter?

PRACTICE

Investing time in practicing the new skills that will get
you to your desired destination in your business will
be well worth it. While you are practicing new skill
sets, also get in the practice of including daily rituals
and habits that make you feel good about yourself and
the progress you are making. Make no mistake about
it; every day you show up, you are getting better.

RELAX

I know this might sound odd, but the best thing you
can do for your new publishing business is taking a
chill pill. Find ways to relax your mind and body—
monthly massages, weekly yoga, daily breathwork.
You get to choose and you know what works best for
you. I create a toolbox for myself and when I find my

shoulders touching my ears and my past creeping in to tell me I can't do it, I reach for a tool. My tools include Rescue Remedy, rose tea, lavender oil, gamma wave meditations, walks in nature, sidewalk chalk, coloring, playing Cornhole with my boys, taking a nap, cooking my favorite dish.

I recommend writing out at least five things that relax you and telling one or two trusted friends to remind you of the toolbox when you start to stress, overthink, or worry.

FOCUS

When you have moments of self-doubt, your mind will race to either the past or the future and neither one will likely feel good. The minute you recognize this, focus on one thing at the moment. It can be a cloud, a painting, the way your shirt feels on your skin, any one thing. Connect to your senses and one thing in your environment and swiftly bring yourself back to center.

ESCAPE

While this might seem as if you should keep facing whatever is making you feel unsure, intimidated, or less then, sometimes our nervous system needs a break. When you feel like this, log out of social media, turn the noise off, and distract yourself with something that allows your system to reach a state of calm. Remember, it is good to remove yourself from situations that continuously put you in fight or flight.

ENCOURAGEMENT

When you experience a difficult day or face disappointment, you need someone on your team. Most people have a great support network but rarely tap into it. Get in the practice of reaching out when you need encouragement and allow yourself to receive love and support. In addition to this, become your own biggest cheerleader. If this is new to you, imagine what you would tell your best friend or child, then tell that to yourself.

Now that you have a plan to back yourself as you move forward it will be much easier, trust me!

The first thing I want you to determine is if your current audience would be a good fit for your book. If you don't have an audience, that's ok, I'll cover what to do soon.

Keep in mind: ideally, they make at least $100k, they have cash flowing, they regularly invest in themselves and they understand the power of networking and marketing themselves.

If you determine that the audience is ideal, the next step is simple: go tell your clients, group, email list, and audience what you are up to and give them an opportunity to say yes to you.

I announced my first multi-author book project in my private Facebook group and immediately sold the first handful of spots. I then went live until the book sold out and 27 women had said yes to telling their story.

If you have cultivated an audience and know they are listening to what you'll offer next, leap. Really, this is going to be a very easy project for you, especially if you have created a title you know speaks right to them.

Now, what if you have an audience lacking this kind of income or used to investing at lower price points? I say put it out there. You have nothing to lose and I have often found that many times an audience will rise to the occasion.

You might need to emphasize more on what the outcome of the book project is and highlight its value. You also might need to do a bit more education, but it will be well worth it.

What if you do not have an audience? Your social

media contacts include your best friend from fourth grade and the other soccer moms; I got you. The beauty of social media is that it gives us access to about a billion people around the world. How amazing is that?

At any time of day or night, you can search for groups based on titles or interests. You can ask a question and learn about new resources. And if you want to get clients quickly without a current audience, I highly recommend networking in other people's groups on Facebook and/or creating 25 or more new connections on LinkedIn.

Remember I said sales is really about talking to people like a woman on a mission until you find the ones who get what you are doing? That is all you need to do; have conversations every day until you find your people.

That either got you very excited or freaked out. Either way, it's good!

I would be lying if I said starting a publishing company will allow you to sit in the back row, watching others be fully self-expressed and taking confident action. Owning a publishing company will highlight all the places that are stuck, suppressed, afraid of rejection, and seeking validation and approval at any cost.

What?!

I know that most people do not have what it takes to grow into this kind of person, but you are different. You are dying to be fully self-expressed and confident in your business and radiate passion in a way that people cannot get close enough because they desire the same.

Here's the raw deal: if we can't get out of our own way, we don't deserve to serve those who are ready to shine their light and use their voice for the good of all.

Audience or no audience, the fastest way to find contributors is to tell everyone what you are up to, who you are looking for, and why it matters. When you start to wonder if anyone is right for you, remember finding 20 or 30 that are a match for your book is very doable in a world of eight billion people.

It is important to make sure you are the kind of woman who believes in herself and her dreams before you take action—and it *will* require action. If you do this time, the algorithms won't matter, the platform won't matter, the past won't matter; the energy that is dripping off you will be the thing that trumps all.

If you still aren't sure where to find clients, be sure to download my checklist, **WHERE YOUR DREAM CLIENTS ARE HIDING IN PLAIN SITE** in the private Facebook group. You can get this once you sign up for my free masterclass:

www.adrianamoniquealvarez.com/how-to-start-your-own-publishing-company

6

How to Make Six Figures from
Your Publishing Company in the
First Year

I should have said this in the opening line of the book; there is no reason to even consider starting your own publishing company if you do not see yourself creating at least $100k a year in it. Whether this is going to be your main business or a side business, make sure you go into this thinking big.

All right, I am going to walk you through the numbers, and if numbers aren't your love language, it's ok; you'll get the idea.

As a general rule, I recommend selling each spot in a multi-author book at US$1000 or more for two reasons:

1. I want you to work with a $20k budget to cover editing, formatting, cover design, administration, and your paycheck.

2. I want you to work with an audience that regularly invests in their personal and professional development. This audience will not think twice about investing US$1000+ to be in your book.

When you keep your pricing at US$1000 or more and you market to the right people, you can forget about:

- Overcoming Objections

I cannot tell you how freeing it was when I stopped handing objections and simply starting allowing people to sort out their issues. It is not your job to assist them with figuring out where the money could come from. They are grown adults and they make buying decisions daily. They either know how to increase their income and how to budget or not. It is also not your job to convince them that being in your book is a great way to market their business and network. They get it or they don't.

- Following Up for Weeks and Months

Now I know this is going to go against what most people teach—what I taught for years—but the best thing I did for my business and sanity was creating irresistible offers with a limited opening and let people jump in or not. The only time I follow up with someone is if we reach an agreement in a conversation but circumstances prevent them from taking action within my time frame. When you follow what I teach, you will never chase after people who have no intention of working with you but find it easier to say, "let me think about it." We all know the last thing they will do is think about it. They are going to jump out of that Zoom room and move on with their life.

- Hearing Money Stories, Excuses, and Drama

The lower the price point, the more likely you will hear all the above. Now you might be thinking, *a thousand bucks isn't high-end*, and you are right. However, it creates a threshold. Now you can further decrease your chances of hearing all sorts of dramatic stories if you choose high-caliber people to feature in your book. People who are in leadership positions, people who have at least three years of experience, and people who have a regular stream of clients are much less likely to complain and waste your time.

When you position your books correctly, market them well, and speak only to successful people who have money to invest in their growth, you are golden.

The best clients are not attracted to low, entry-level price points so when Sally Sue says, "well I know of another book that is offering spots for $300," you can easily say, "I completely understand, this is not right for you because it's not."

If you would like to create a lucrative recession-proof business, it is critical to only market to those who are not negatively impacted by fluctuating economies. These people have...

- SAVINGS
- INVESTMENTS
- MULTIPLE STREAMS OF INCOME

...and maybe the most important of all, they can adapt and make more money in down markets.

If you are going to make $100k or more in your first year and expand from there, it is key that you never, ever, ever market to broke people with loads of potential.

This is not a charity; this is a business.

If these numbers have you all kinds of sideways and you feel like I am a jerk for saying that the only people who belong in your book make a certain amount of money, you might want to look at how you feel about money and how comfortable you are receiving it.

You almost might want to ask yourself if you are ready to be the CEO of a successful company and make wise business decisions because, without these, you won't be able to take care of your family, much less give back to people and causes you care about.

All right, enough of that. Let's look at numbers!

There are two main ways to profit from each multi-author book: front end and back end.

Front end money is the fee you charge to participate in the book ($1000+).

Back end money is the up-sells you offer after the book reaches bestseller status (services, products, retreats, solo books).

I teach my clients to set the intention of making at least $15k profit on the front end of the book and at least $35k profit on the back end. Keep in mind my clients can produce books for $4k-$5k each because I introduce them to my team and we also have trainers that offer this as a done-for-you service so you do not need to worry about interviewing, hiring, and managing an entire team.

This means you take home about $50k per multi-author book your publishing house produces. Now consider how many books you would like to produce a year and multiply it out.

How much income would you like to create over the next 12 months through your publishing company?

Would that amount be worth it for you to learn the structure, skill sets, and strategies for sure success?

Now, every woman does this slightly differently and you will too. Some of my clients charge $1500 for each spot in their book and they take 30 contributors per book. That gives them $45k in upfront money minus the $5k to produce the book, so they are profiting $40k from the participation fee.

Other clients have two price points to participate in: a regular fee and a VIP option. This allows them to make twice as much on each spot sold.

Other clients are very good at up-sells. For example, in my first book, I offered a networking training at $399 and sold 41 spots for a total of $16,359 and then I offered a $15k coaching package and sold three for a total of $45k. The back end money on that book was $61,359.

One of my clients got three solo authors after her multi-author book hit bestseller status. She sold each spot for $12k for a total of $36k.

Keep in mind that you do not need to be a business coach to have a great up-sell. My clients come from a variety of backgrounds and it is ideal to select services, products, or experiences that are in your wheelhouse.

It is that simple. Now you know how to map out a six-figure year for your publishing company.

All you need to do now is look at how you work best.

We offer three ways to work with us: private coaching, a group program, and a home study course.

Our private coaching is ideal for the woman who is drained by a group program, moves quickly, and desires to make $250k or more a year. She also might have other businesses that we need to integrate with the publishing house.

Our group program is perfect for the woman who is motivated by a group, thrives in a supportive community, and desires to make $100k or more a year.

And our home study course is designed for the woman who loves learning on her own, is self-disciplined, and a finisher.

What are your financial goals for your publishing house? We would love for you to share them in the private Facebook group. Sign up for my free masterclass and join the group:

www.adrianamoniquealvarez.com/how-to-start-your-own-publishing-company

7

How to Build an International Enterprise

*C*ongrats on getting this far! The last thing I want to share with you is the importance of building an international enterprise. When Derek and I started our business many moons ago, right in the middle of a real estate market crash and all the followed, I had no idea we would create an international business.

We were local. I attended Chamber events, BNI breakfasts, and that was all I knew. What drove me online was two-fold, having two babies in twelve months and my desire to travel with my family. I had to expand. Having a local business, a regional business, even a national business, is most likely not going to support the vision and desires that are burning in your bones. I wish someone would have told me that I could have an international business and to think like that from the beginning. That is why I telling you.

It all starts with a decision and then there are a few actions that you can take to back this decision.

I remember the first event where I was vocal about bringing in people from at least 20 countries. I had no idea how it was going to happen, but I went live every day and talked about the four-week networking event I was creating, the benefits, and that I wanted women from all over the world. I did one small thing that made a big difference — I included four major timezones in my marketing so that women could see I was taking timezones into consideration and I was hosting the event in a way that everyone could participate.

I had 111 women register from 23 different countries and that was when I was hooked!

Having an international empire brings in a richness that cannot otherwise be achieved. When a wide range of backgrounds, cultures, and experiences collaborate, everyone is better for it. It also taught me timezones (I am still getting there honestly), it showed me the strengths of each region, and what the common threads are no matter where we come from.

After that event, I had one client in Australia and she was amazing. I got the idea that I wanted more

Australian clients so I joined a large Facebook group with an Aussie admin. I posted regularly, told great stories, taught and trained like they were all paying clients and within six months over 60 of them were.

Then Derek and I made a trip to Australia so I could meet some of my clients and take them out to dinner. The bond was strengthened, and now Australia makes up 60% of my total business.

I have now worked with clients in 36 countries and I have learned so much from every single one!

There are benefits to having an international clientele when it comes to publishing as well. The first book I released had contributors from eight countries and we hit bestseller status in them all.

Getting our books in hands around the world feels amazing!

And telling your clients that are INTERNATIONAL BESTSELLING AUTHORS… well there is nothing better. So, I invite you to think big and take actions that lead you to receive clients from around the world.

If you don't yet have a global business, I invite you to take these simple steps to set the stage:

1. Participate in groups with admins in countries and regions outside of where you live or are from.
2. When you go live or host an event, post several time zones — not only the one you live in.
3. Find affiliates and brand ambassadors outside your home country.
4. Make it clear that you desire to work with clients from around the world.
5. Host events at a variety of times so you can accommodate people no matter where they live.

Last but not least, if you are from a part of the world where people would be unable to invest at the level I teach, due to the currency exchange, having an international business is going to be even more important for you.

Are you ready to start your own high-impact publishing house? Be sure to join the private Facebook group to see what kind of special offers we might be running. You can join the group once you sign up for my free masterclass:

www.adrianamoniquealvarez.com/how-to-start-your-own-publishing-company

8

Success Stories

*I*n this section, I want to introduce you to women who have made at least $8k in their publishing house.

They will share with you what their background and previous experience included, why they chose to start their publishing house, their favorite marketing method for selling spots in their book, and the biggest way they have grown since becoming the CEO of their publishing house. Be sure to check out their websites and groups, these women are doing incredible work and leading the way.

COLLEEN REAGAN NOON

My name is Colleen Reagan Noon, and I started my publishing house, Wise Women Book Collective, in 2020. Before starting my publishing business, I was a birth and parenting educator. I helped empower parents to evolve into their higher selves. By processing their traumas and thought patterns, parents can then step into their roles in a more profound way that radiates through the family. One of the best ways that I have found to help people process trauma, big and little, and create new thought patterns is through writing. It was an obvious transition for me to move into book publishing as this is such an amazing platform for personal transformation on different levels.

I didn't have a vast network when I opened my publishing house. In essence, I felt as if I was starting from zero. My previous clients weren't the target clients for this business, which put me in a place where I had to call in the right people. Targeted reach outs through LinkedIn ended up being the route to success for my first book. The books that followed were filled easily through referrals from the authors in my first book. All I needed was the effort to push that first domino, and then the rest have fallen beautifully to create a business that will undoubtedly bring in over $100k in my first year.

I never thought of myself as ever being a CEO but a stay-at-home mom with a business on the side. When my business up-leveled, it up-leveled me as well. I still had one of my children home full time, but my thoughts, actions, and what I spent my time doing all changed. My business pulled me up to a place where I had no choice but to hire a bookkeeper, an email list manager, someone to do my website, and others. I was no longer doing it all, and I had the capital to make it all work. I enjoy holding the reins to my business. It goes where I lead it, and there is no limit to what I can do or what I can earn. It's a freedom unlike anything else I have ever experienced.

I was attracted to this opportunity right away. Something deep inside me saw the potential for working with people in a way I loved while also providing a better income for my family. I followed my heart, and it led me to a place that I could never have imagined. It's a place that I have always been destined to be.

ABOUT COLLEEN

Colleen Reagan Noon is the founder of Wise Women Book Collective. She empowers women to share their wisdom and expand their impact by becoming best-selling authors. Colleen publishes multi-author books under her publishing name and offers publishing services to other female-owned publishers and authors. Colleen is an international bestselling author five times over and has helped over 35 people become bestselling authors. Before founding her company, she was an educator working with young children and their parents. She focused on teaching parents about birth, trauma recovery, and parenting while in substance abuse recovery. She continues to be an advocate for parents in substance abuse recovery and their spouses.

Colleen is a mother of two and considers New York, Massachusetts, and Florida all home. She received her B.A. at Rollins College in Winter Park, FL, and her M. Ed at Lesley University in Cambridge, MA.

To date, Colleen has made nearly $50k from starting her own publishing house. You can find her at *www.wisewomenbookco.com* where she helps both authors and publishers get their works out into the world.

KAYLEIGH O'KEEFE

Soul Excellence Publishing for Business Leaders

Hi! I'm Kayleigh O'Keefe, and I am the founder of Soul Excellence Publishing, the publishing house for courageous, conscious leaders.

We work exclusively with executives and entrepreneurs who want to share their stories of personal transformation, but don't have the time to write a full book or manage the intricacies of self-publishing.

I believe that information is everywhere, but wisdom is scarce.

I founded the company in September 2020 after a 13-year career in corporate America. My background includes over eight years as a management research consultant where I worked with Fortune 500 executives in the sales, marketing, and communications space. I also spent nearly four years in early-stage technology companies in San Francisco, where I built out new product lines and commercial teams as we scaled. There's nothing like sensing a need, rallying a team behind a solution, and taking daily aligned action to achieve something monumental!

I had also experienced the joy of becoming a bestselling author in the book *Awakening* in Spring of 2020, and it opened my eyes to achieving my dreams in collaboration with others. I had always wanted to write a book, and it was amazing to me that I could accomplish this by writing a chapter, aligning with a great topic, and supporting other women in the process. It helped me to experience what I would soon offer other executives out there who were tired of going it alone or "doing it all by themselves."

Why Soul Excellence Publishing Now

From a young age, I've always enjoyed reading, writing, speaking, and immersing myself in the world of ideas. In eighth grade, I loved broadcasting local and school sports scores on the morning TV announcements! Later, I would go on to be the speaker at my undergraduate and business school commencements. Expressing my ideas and energizing others have always been important to me. When the concept of Soul Excellence Leadership came into my awareness, I knew that I wanted to create a new platform for leaders to come together to write, express, and share ideas.

I felt even more called to start my publishing

company in 2020 when I saw how much online censorship is happening and how narrow the bounds of free speech and expression have become in a narrative-driven and social-media-influenced world. It is my mission to enable more people to live joyously, which I believe can only happen when we all feel free to share our ideas, opinions, and perspectives and also have the mental and emotional intelligence to discern the truth.

LinkedIn and Virtual Leadership Summits

Our authors are primarily business executives, and they live on LinkedIn where their professional reputation lives. To recruit for our first book, *Leading Through the Pandemic: Unconventional Wisdom from Heartfelt Leaders*, I used LinkedIn Sales Navigator to send connection requests to leaders above the VP level in a variety of geographies. Once they accepted my request, I asked if they wanted to participate in the book. I then had them fill out a simple application form to see if they were a strong fit for the project.

To fill our second multi-author book, I used a similar technique, and we also benefited from holding our leadership summit for Leading Through the Pandemic on Facebook. During the Summit where I interviewed the authors, I put out the invitation to participants to apply for our next book, *Significant Women.* It was extremely powerful for potential authors to hear how transformative the experience working with me and my team had been from the current authors.

Becoming a CEO

I've grown tremendously since founding my company. I had never been an entrepreneur before launching Soul Excellence Publishing. It's one thing to advise executives as a consultant and partner with a CEO to build a company and it's a whole different thing to commit to yourself and your vision as the CEO of your own company. Founding Soul Excellence Publishing gave me confidence that my decision to leave corporate and chart my own course was right for me.

We're Just Getting Started

My publishing company generated over $75k in our first six months. Just as important, we've helped over 45 executives become international bestselling authors, which has helped them to increase their visibility, expand their financial and career opportunities, and connect with new networks around the world.

ABOUT KAYLEIGH

Kayleigh Marie O'Keefe is the CEO and founder of Soul Excellence Publishing where she helps corporate leaders and entrepreneurs build credibility, attract new opportunities, and leave a legacy through multi-author books, solo books, and ghostwriting.

The company's multi-author leadership books, *Leading Through the Pandemic: Unconventional Wisdom from Heartfelt Leaders* and *Significant Women: Leaders Reveal What Matters Most*, both reached Amazon international bestseller status across key business categories. She also works with leaders who want to expand their impact and influence, attract new opportunities with ease, and create a more fulfilling life using her signature Soul Excellence Leadership framework.

Prior to founding the company, Kayleigh spent nearly a decade as a researcher and consultant for Fortune 500 communications executives with CEB (now Gartner) and as sales and customer success leader at Snapdocs, a Series-C real estate technology company backed by Sequoia Capital and Y Combinator Continuity Fund. She received her B.A. from Duke University and her M.B.A. on a full scholarship from the University of San Francisco.

Connect with her on LinkedIn:
www.linkedin.com/in/kayleighokeefe

BRIGID HOLDER

I am Brigid Holder, the CEO and founder of *The Art of Grace Publishing House* and director of a successful traditional business all based in our small rural town in Cootamundra, NSW, Australia. My corporate background saw me lead companies from 450 to over 4000 clients and from $100K turnover to over $1M, with the support of teams that I created. The publishing company saw me finally find my passion in life – sharing women's stories to impact the lives of others.

Starting the publishing company was as if I was sent a gift from the gods! I had previously contributed to two multi-author books and was set to do more. When the opportunity arose, I grabbed it with both hands and it was as a complete and embodied YES to this new venture.

I love enrolling women into my books and programs via video, both live and recorded. Facebook is where I do 99% of my marketing, with a small portion via my website. I'm not fond of email, but I am getting used to the idea—it is part of the plan moving forward.

Growth has been exponential for me, finding that my zone of genius is in bringing women together into a community, creating a safe container for which they can expand, holding them as they launch into the world, and finding collaboration beyond a book. I also found growth in delegation with online contractors. Not holding control within a traditional bricks-and-mortar office was strange at first but now seems so normal and efficient! I also grew in acceptance of who I am, got more comfortable with me, showed up more as myself. In turn, this has attracted the right women for me to work with. However, my greatest growth has been in going from seeing life with limits to seeing it is now unlimited as to what I can achieve and that I can do it how it suits me!

Numbers, I love numbers....

When I began my journey as a publisher I had little to no idea of the impact of visibility and this is one of the main things I have seen change in a short amount of time.

2400 odd friends online, this grew to 5000 very quickly—having to cull regularly

420 followers to over 900—who regularly comment and give me support

28 women in my first multi-author book gathered over the Christmas holidays

7 women in the solo book group program

3 solo book deals have been sealed

25 women will join me in the motherhood book

25 more successful women will join the next book

8 multi-author books will be published by The Art of Grace Publishing House

We are well on our way to achieve our mission to share the stories of at least 180 women this calendar year, and on track to burst through the $150k turnover that I set to achieve in year one of business.

For me, publishing is not just about books; it's about the art of writing and the Grace in which we can deliver this to the world are the gifts to both the writer and the readers.

ABOUT BRIGID

A successful businesswoman in the traditional sense, Brigid spent about 7 years searching for her passion, and venturing into publishing saw her thrive!

As the CEO of The Art of Grace Publishing House, Brigid sees the power in collaboration, community, and raising the voices of other women to change the world. You can see her often interviewing and championing other women on her Facebook profile. To date, the publishing house has produced $50k in sales.

A two-time international bestselling author herself, Brigid fully understands the power of writing and publishing your work.

Brigid is the mother of two teenage boys and has a passion for the snow and mountains and resides in the rural town of Cootamundra, NSW, Australia, with her husband.

You can find Brigid via *www.brigidholder.com* where all her current projects and links to her books and those of her publishing house can be found.

TARSH ASHWIN

I decided to open up my publishing company in September 2020. Even though I was already running a successful business as a business strategist for online entrepreneurs, I founded Ashwin Publishing because I desired to provide a platform for my clients to share their (oftentimes disruptive and controversial) messages on the global stage. I had experienced firsthand the impact that censorship can have on a business and realized that we cannot rely on traditional social media marketing to grow our businesses and find our tribe. I had also co-authored two multi-author book projects with Adriana who had supported me to finally crack the six-figure ceiling I'd been aiming at for so long.

Establishing a publishing company was such a no-brainer for me.

Since September, I have launched two multi-author books, am marketing the third one, and have just begun working with a client on solo book publishing, bringing in a total of $80k in revenue into the front end of my business.

I've experimented with many different marketing methods. The strategies that have helped me sell out my books include a combination of written content, live video, and referrals. This magic strategy combination has had me sell out books quickly and joyfully.

This has been such a powerful addition to my business and I have grown in many ways since becoming the CEO of Ashwin Publishing. I've attracted over 70 new clients into my sales vortex —many of whom have gone on to invest in my private and group coaching programs.

I have stepped into a new state of professionalism and feel that I can command a more potent energy of authority. I've been able to combine my experience with business strategy and marketing to help my clients achieve fantastic results through participating in my books. As a result, they have consistently referred new authors to me which has helped me fill upcoming books with ease.

ABOUT TARSH

Tarsh is an international bestselling author, business strategist, and the CEO and founder of Ashwin Publishing. She provides a platform for conscious leaders and entrepreneurs to share their message with the world and elevate their authority to strategically bring more profit into their business.

She specializes in guiding soulful women in business to grow their impact-driven business and step into empowered leadership. Her work is a bespoke fusion of energetic transformation and outer strategy implementation that paves the way to purposeful profit. She believes in the incredible power of publishing to grow heart-centered businesses that are committed to effecting transformational global change.

Tarsh lives in Newcastle, Australia, with her partner and two young boys.

www.tarshashwin.com

KRYSTAL HILLE

The Power of Connection and Collaboration

The opportunity to create Krystal Hille Publishing came at a time when my existing events business was forced to shut down due to the COVID-19 pandemic.

I was in and out of planes, flying across Australia to facilitate tantric temple nights, connecting participants deeply with their bodies, their truth, self-love, bliss, and others authentically.

Working as a tantric facilitator had been the natural next step in my ten-year coaching practice where I had primarily worked with women to awaken their feminine essence. Now it was time to enable my clients to step into a deeper sense of embodiment and inner union.

To step up my business, I had just rebranded my company to work with conscious leaders because I knew that to make a big impact on the advancement of humanity, I had to guide leaders into their highest potential.

When publishing presented, a 30-year life circle was completed. At 17, I was the editor of my school magazine, went on to study English Literature, and then brought the stories of literature alive on stage as a theatre director. Next, I was ready to guide clients to transform their life stories from mediocre to magnificent. With publishing, I hold space for leaders to tap into the transformative power of their stories to inspire readers to see their lives through the eyes of another. I guide my contributors to expand into the next level of their leadership and impact.

I've become aware that I am here to assist humanity's to transition into a new era. This is the time of collective leadership and connecting with other leaders, aligned with the same mission. Creating books became the vehicle for us all to unite.

Krystal Hille Publishing's mission is to awaken and empower humanity into deeper connection and sovereignty through the power of stories and the embodied wisdom of visionaries, way-showers, and successful leaders.

The power of connection and collaboration became my absolute favorite way to share the opportunity to join my books, where I am offering solutions to a visibility problem.

I went through the many online summits I had been a part of over the last five years and approached my peers who had spoken alongside me. I contacted them directly and as we had something in common, I had instant credibility, even though I had never published a book.

My second favorite marketing tool is creating relationships with powerhouse referrers—those who are mentoring ideal clients for my books. By paying a referral fee, it became a nice incentive for my peers to also reach out to their colleagues and clients. Within six weeks, the first book was sold out.

Yes, there were challenges. The universe made sure I had many growing opportunities to become the best CEO of my publishing house I could be. In the past, I had experienced a perennial limit of eight participants in any group program I held. This time, I made a promise to find 25, and I had to keep that promise, no matter what.

My first book was called 'Fearless Presence'. Now I had to stand in my fearless presence if I was going to get the remaining contributors into that book. I made a list of all the things I was scared of and much surfaced to be embraced and transmuted around legal threats, court costs, and health. The minute I was at peace with all worst-case scenarios, the flood gates opened and the remaining contributors joined.

At the time of writing, the chapters for my first book are flooding in, and my second book, *COLLABORATION: How to Release the Paradigm of Competition'* has been conceived.

ABOUT KRYSTAL

Krystal Hille is a Soul Leadership coach, Tantra teacher, and CEO of Krystal Hille Publishing, where she shares stories that inspire the evolution and empowerment of humanity.

She works with conscious leaders to embody their soul essence, claim their gifts and realize their visions through mentoring and creating bestseller multi-author books, increasing her clients' reach, impact and influence.

With 30 years in leadership, a background in theatre directing, and female empowerment, Krystal hosts the Soul Leadership Podcast, is a Brainz Magazine executive contributor, and author of multiple international bestsellers. She is regularly invited to present at online summits and festivals. Aware of her multi-dimensional self, she is passionate to bring the divine feminine codes back to this planet, guiding humanity into sovereignty, unity, and grace. She is also the founder of the Galactic Temple, an online membership portal with bi-monthly activation gatherings.

www.krystalhille.com/publishing

≈

BRIDGET AILEEN SICSKO

Exalted Publishing House

Prior to starting my own publishing company, I had zero—and I repeat, zero—experience in the publishing industry. My prior experience was in sales, advertising, coaching, podcasting, and healing.

My background probably sounds a lot like the typical entrepreneur—non-linear and quite a meandering journey. After graduating from college with a Digital Communications and Organizational Leadership degree, I began working in advertising sales for Yelp. Realizing quite quickly that was not the path for me, I quit my job, traveled to Europe, and studied Yoga and Ayurveda in Ibiza, Spain. During that time, I began to reflect on my Lymes disease journey starting at age 15. When I was younger, I felt so frustrated—sick of endless rounds of antibiotics which never got to the root of the illness and felt unheard by the doctors who were meant to help me. I knew that experience was a clue to my mission and I wanted to make sure all voices were heard.

When I returned home from Europe, I began teaching yoga and became a certified holistic health coach. Over those years, I worked with autistic young adults, healers, veterans, alcoholics, children and the message again became very clear to me: I was here to hear people's stories and remind them that they are never alone. As my work began to transition into serving female entrepreneurs - the message remained, just in a different way. I started to help successful female entrepreneurs find their voice, craft their message and use it strategically to become more visible online. To this day, my experience has seamlessly, albeit not always easily, paved the way for my work in the world now and taught me I was ready to start a publishing company.

The decision to start a publishing house was one of the easiest decisions for me. Business-wise, my mission was rock-solid. I was here to amplify the voices of powerful leaders, change-makers, and entrepreneurs. At this time, I already had a podcast, *The Gathering MVMT,* where I interviewed these leaders who were here to make a difference in the world. In addition, my coaching business was growing rapidly. I had just pivoted my focus to be on successful, spiritual female entrepreneurs who wanted to master the art of live video, public speaking and refine their message for upcoming launches. The dots were already connecting. When the publishing company opportunity was presented to me, I thought "holy crow, this is the missing piece of my puzzle".

My favorite way to sell spots in my book is through live video. It is the most natural way, in my opinion, to truly and deeply connect with my community. Live video allows someone to know me, see me, hear me, and most importantly from a marketing perspective, trust me. I create one incredible live video and send all book applicants to my live video. In addition, I create more videos throughout the launch process to teach on things like how to monetize their book, why networking is the new advertising, and how writing a book helps you get booked on podcasts.

I feel like an entirely new woman since opening

my publishing company. I am 27 years old, hiring a team of experts to help me facilitate, organize, edit, publish and format my books. My vision for my business and the direction I want this business to go in could not be more clear. Monetarily, I am earning more than I was in the past, so I have the foundation to truly scale and grow now. Most importantly, I am a woman with a plan now. I have made more than $25k in my publishing business.

ABOUT BRIDGET

Bridget Aileen Sicsko is the founder of Exalted Publishing House, a podcast host and sales and messaging coach. She helps successful entrepreneurs stand out and be featured as a leader in their industry through sharing powerful stories. Her mission is to amplify the voices of powerful entrepreneurs who are ready to elevate their business, become published authors and public speakers. Bridget also hosts a live interview series called "The Gathering MVMT" where she has interviewed over 40 entrepreneurs, TedX speakers, authors, thought-leaders, and visionaries who are here to uplift humanity. She lives in New Jersey with her husband and her dog, Finn.

www.bridgetaileen.com

LEANNE CLUNE

I am Leanne Clune, CEO of Leanne Clune and Co and Clune & Co Publishing. I have run a successful finance company for the last 16 years, saving hundreds of clients millions of dollars collectively.

My soul mission is to increase the cashflow of the leading visionary entrepreneurs in this world. This enables them to invest more in themselves and their business, expand their reach and income and lift more people with them. It creates a beautiful, high-frequency ripple effect.

In mid-2020, I committed to writing in a multi-author book for the first time. This was one of the best business decisions I have ever made. My business revenue tripled as a direct result of the exponential marketing of the book. A few months later, every cell in my body said yes to adding a publishing arm to my finance business.

Before I contributed to a bestselling book, I didn't think my stories would be interesting to many people. I actually thought my life was quite 'normal'. Interestingly, I can always see my client's story's so clearly. I would often tell my clients they need to write a book. Working with clients on a deep financial level leaves no room for secrets!

Once I started brainstorming for my story, it was like opening the flood gates. I had hundreds of stories to tell and I was ready to tell them. This became my favorite marketing tool for my book, *Radiante - Visionary Women Igniting the Light in Others*. I told my stories on social media in lives and written form.

I explained my vision for my book and clearly articulated the types of women I was looking for. I magnetically attracted the ones that resonated with my vision. It took some time to start the momentum. I was still embodying my new role as CEO of my own publishing company.

What the heck! I never thought I would own a publishing house!

Personally, since taking on this publishing company, I cannot recognize my old self. The transformations were rapid and ongoing. Initially, they were painful and I had to give my body time to integrate them. My whole body was re-wiring to manage the new frequency required to do this. During this process, I also transitioned a huge component of my business to online. It required massive learning and upskilling. I had always worked in a more traditional method but the need to transition had been calling for years.

Establishing a publishing company has been one of the best decisions I have ever made in my business. I have established strong connections with leading businesswomen from all over the globe. I am so proud of what I have created and it is only the beginning.

ABOUT LEANNE

Leanne Clune is an international best-selling author, cashflow coach and CEO and facilitator of the Radiante series of multi-author books. She helps soulful, change maker, female entrepreneurs rid themselves of old patterns, stories and beliefs to activate their inner wealth magnetism. This allows them to catapult their cashflow and manifest a new financial reality for themselves.

With over 15 year's experience running her own finance company, she has helped hundreds of clients save millions of dollars collectively. Her experience led her to see the limitations in the traditional finance systems, especially for women. This led her to create several cashflow transformation programs including

Creative Energetic Millionaires and Amplifying Abundance.

Leanne lives with her husband and three sons on one acre of tropical paradise in the Gold Coast Hinterland.

www.facebook.com/leannecluneco

TARRYN REEVES

Four Eagles Publishing & The Publishing House Concierge

I went to university and got a Bachelor of Criminology. Whilst I was studying, I got a job in the railway as an operations support officer. I spent five years in the railway, moving up the corporate ladder and adding to my skillset of logistics, systems and procedures, people management, and conflict resolution. Turns out a corporate career like that did not fit who I was and I burnt out spectacularly. I got a part-time job doing the rostering in a not-for-profit but was made redundant a week before I found out I was pregnant. Tired of being at the mercy of heartless corporations I decided to start my own business as a virtual assistant. I quickly scaled that business up to a virtual assistance and web development agency. I then added a business coaching element to my business. After I had booked my calendar solid with 1:1 coaching clients, I began to look at other ways to scale my business and my income.

I decided to start my own publishing house as it just made sense to me. Here was a proven method of making money that would fit seamlessly in with my other business elements. I have always been a lover of books and being able to work with them for a living. . . well sign me up! I also experienced first-hand the power of a book when used as a strategic marketing tool for business. I also realized that I had a natural talent for distilling stories into potent marketing tools and teaching high-level coaches how to grow their business on autopilot. Starting my own publishing house is the best decision I have made for my business to date, both personally and professionally. I have never been happier in my business and am making more money, more easily than ever before.

Favorite method for selling spots in my book

My favorite method for selling spots in my multi-author book projects is a lead generation campaign that I developed, which can be outsourced to a virtual assistant and takes very little of my time. It works a little something like this:

Know your ideal client

Choose a social media platform such as LinkedIn

Find your ideal clients using the search tool

Reach out to them and schedule a call to tell them more about the project

I hear lots of no's, but I also hear lots of yes's.

The biggest way I have grown since becoming the CEO of my publishing house

I have grown in so many ways since saying yes to becoming the CEO of my own publishing house but if I had to pick one I would say it is my self-confidence. I finally feel like I have found my spot in the world. I was making money before, lots of it, but something always felt like it was missing. I don't feel that way anymore. I wake up every day inspired and on purpose. I have so much more energy for life and I adore what I do and the people I get to do it with. Since starting my publishing house, I have made $50k+.

ABOUT TARRYN

Tarryn Reeves is the CEO and founder of Four Eagles Publishing and The Publishing House Concierge.

She works with high-level coaches to create best-selling books that multiply their business on autopilot. Her specialty is creating an amazing reader experience that converts book sales into clients.

She is an international bestselling author and has a global client base. She resides in Australia with her husband and daughter. When she isn't creating best-sellers, she is scouring the local book shares to add to her collection.

You can connect with Tarryn at:

www.tarrynreeves.com

ANNETTE MARIA SZPROCH

My name is Annette Maria Szproch and I'm the founder of Sanctuary Publishing. Prior to birthing Sanctuary Publishing, I was in healing and coaching work from yoga teaching, massaging to embodiment coaching. Alongside my publishing house, I facilitate deep healing work through Purpose Embodiment Coaching where I support women to connect to their Feminine essence and find safety within themselves to expand to live out their soul's purpose.

Writing and storytelling is a healing process in itself which is why I decided to infuse Sanctuary Publishing into my business. Sanctuary Publishing was founded on allowing individuals to feel wildly expressed in who they are while living out their purpose. I support soulpreneurs through multi-author and solo-author books to create a deep impact and increase their income.

I started my publishing house in March 2021 and within one month, I have made $20k+. In one month, I created more income than my business has ever seen and the possibilities truly feel like they have opened up for me for greater abundance! The way I connected and sold spots within my books was through cold messaging and referrals. I love sincere connection and that is how I treated my cold outreach, as a genuine invitation to the human on the other side.

Through becoming a CEO of Sanctuary Publishing, I have stepped into a role of leadership I have been deeply yearning for. It has allowed me to own the powerful woman that I truly am through managing a team and creating sacred experiences for others. It has also taken the pressure off my healing work and allowed it to have space to breathe rather than pressure to fill my healing schedule.

The opportunity to start a publishing house came at the perfect time and I'm so grateful that I took the leap into making this happen for myself. Through stepping into this, I truly feel anything is possible for my business.

ABOUT ANNETTE

Annette Maria is the founder of Sanctuary Publishing where she supports soulpreneurs in the process of sharing their empowering story. She curates multi-author and solo-author books. Alongside Sanctuary Publishing she is a Purpose Embodiment coach, intuitive facilitator of healing, a channel for multi-dimensional beings, host of Sacred Dance Podcast, and published author, Bhakti Yogi. Her work guides women from burnt out warriors to purpose-driven goddesses. She wants to see the planet a place that supports everyone feeling wildly expressed in their soul's purpose, reminded of their limitless potential, and able to fully feel their humanness. She resides in New Jersey with her artist partner, George, and rescue dog, Max.

You can connect with Annette to support you in feeling wildly expressed through becoming a published author or supporting you within your healing journey, Check her out at *www.annettemaria.org*

DR. PATRICIA SUGGS

PKS Publishing

My journey has been a circuitous one. For 43 years, I was in ministry in the United Methodist Church, where I served churches for some of those years. For 17 of those years, I was an associate professor in Geriatrics at Wake Forest University School of Medicine. I developed curriculum and trained health providers on how to deal with their aging patients and clients. I am an International Coaching Federation certified coach, and I am certified in Conflict Resolution. I have worked with numerous groups and individuals helping them learn how to address difficult situations both personally and professionally.

I have coached for several years in the areas of personal and leadership development, conflict resolution, communication skills and techniques, and the role of spirituality in personal and professional lives. My niche is professional women. I inspire them to stand up and stand out in their career so they gain visibility, are heard and see an increase in their income and in promotions.

When I received the opportunity to start a

publishing house, I realized that this was an excellent means by which I could reach large numbers of women with stories by other women and myself. This goes hand in hand with my coaching business. There was one drawback: while I love books, I knew nothing about publishing! That is where Adriana Monique Alvarez and her training came in. I learned what I needed to know to put together multi-author and solo books and make them bestsellers.

This has been an amazing journey! I can't begin to explain the huge learning curve I had to go through. I had never done anything like this before. To be totally honest, it was frustrating at times and I wasn't always sure I would make it. However, I was very determined, and giving up was not an option. While it was hard for me at times it was well worth the effort. What a fabulous ride it was!! And it actually became fun!

My first book, *ASPIRE: Women Finding Their Purpose*, will launch on April 30, 2021. My second multi-author book, *INVISIBLE NO MORE: From the Darkness of Discrimination to the Light of Success, Women Speak Out*, is in the gathering of authors phase. I am looking for women who have experienced some type of bias/discrimination but have worked through it to become successful and are ready to tell their stories to help other women do the same. For those interested, more information is given below.

I have grown tremendously since starting my publishing company. I have taken on a stronger leadership role. I am more confident in my leadership abilities and far more willing to put myself out there. I love the women I am meeting and the stories they have to tell. I have ventured way out of my comfort zone. In my career(s) for 43 years, I didn't have to really 'market' myself. This was totally new. But I learned and earned over $20k in the process.

Some ask why I didn't just retire and do whatever I wanted. Because I believe I am not done yet. I have a burning fire in my belly to help women rise to their greatness. My dream is to start a movement where women rise and enable others to rise, and on and on.... The time for women to fulfill their purposes and be all they were created to be is now. NOW is our time. And I want to help make that happen. Publishing books through my own company will help me achieve that.

ABOUT PATRICIA

Dr. Patricia Suggs is an international bestselling author, CEO of PKS Publishing, and founder of Patricia Suggs Coaching. She is known for her ability to teach women how to find their voice, step into leadership, and excel at conflict resolution. She has announced her new program for professional women: The Success Formula to Stand Out in Your Career.

Currently, she is taking applications for her new multi-author book: INVISIBLE NO MORE: From the Darkness of Discrimination to the Light of Success, Women Speak Out. Email Dr. Suggs for the application.

She resides in Pfafftown, NC with her husband, 3 dogs, 1 rabbit, and 4 ducks.

Email: *pksuggs@gmail.com*
Website: *www.pksuggscoaching.com*

ELEONOR AMORA MARKLUND

Media House of Sovereignty with Publishing House of Sovereignty and UNFUCK Publishing

After contributing several chapters to multi-author books, I found the process of writing my story to be a cathartic and healing experience with the potential of creating profound change. As leaders and influencers, we're driven to do our part to elevate the vibration of the entire planet. We know that it is our birthright to thrive in a reality of freedom in every aspect of our lives. I 'm here to show my proteges that their true path means no more giving away their power, no more believing that they are small and helpless. You have the power to take charge of your life, understand your reincarnation and fulfilling your responsibility to the collective awakening. My publishing houses provides the support people need to step up to the plate and tell their story.

The bulk of my contributors have come from my existing audience and clientele who are entrepreneurs primed to take advantage of the networking and business opportunities available to those who contribute to a multi-author book. I have modeled for them what is possible when you leverage your voice, and they are eager to tap into the healing potential of telling their story to a global audience. Nothing makes me prouder than when my contributors show up with courage to own their past including the wounds and glory, so they can authentically tell their full story.

What started off as a one-woman show has turned into a team spanning the globe. The House of Sovereignty multiplex enterprise is committed to changing lives through exponentially expanding and strengthening my community of spiritual rebels through the various arms of my business. Since adding the publishing arm to my business, I gained significant momentum in evolving my branding, business offerings, revenue, and global impact. This exposure has helped me to become an even bigger authority in my field of expertise. My first publishing house has developed into a full-fledged media wing that houses both UNFUCK Publishing and the Publishing House of Sovereignty which continue to enjoy rapid growth and expansion. I am creating a global empire with far reaching impact and influence.

ABOUT ELEONOR

Eleonor Amora Marklund is an internationally acclaimed expert in energy healing, highly esteemed as the forefront coach for spiritual warriors known as Indigos. Renowned for her groundbreaking work in esotericism, Eleonor is an award-winning international best-selling author who has published over ten bestsellers.

With over 25 years of experience as a therapist, Eleonor's been featured for her authority on energy work and the Indigo awakening on television, podcasts, radio, and in magazines. Her award-winning publications on the intersection of woman-hood, entrepreneurship, and metaphysics have achieved critical acclaim.

As a spiritual philanthropist and innovator, Eleonor founded the House of Sovereignty multiplex enterprise where she is committed to changing lives through exponentially expanding and strengthening her community of spiritual rebels. Her publishing and media arms help readers connect to the Universe and their consciousness on a deeper level.

www.eleonoramora.com

JESSICA VERRILL

I'm Jessica Verrill and I founded House of Indigo, a publishing house, in February 2021. My previous focus was as an intuitive and energy coach. I worked with clients through an energetic and mindset lens to develop their connection to themselves, release anything holding them back and to utilize that power in their lives and businesses. The processes would typically lead to more depth, gratitude and enjoyment within all aspects of life. While my work was extremely rewarding, it felt limiting in the amount of impact and those I could serve with the one-to-one or small group model. I also knew that my expertise was incredibly transformative for many, but not for all. The ability to amplify the voices of other incredible purpose-driven entrepreneurs and businesses through publishing has allowed me and all of my authors the ability to massively expand our impact.

When I branched out with House of Indigo, I had taken a huge leap of faith and felt an alignment with my work at a level I had yet to experience. The glimpses of future timelines I had viewed all began to make sense, and I went all in. I felt behind the mark sometimes; I didn't have an email list of thousands to fall back upon, a fancy funnel system or even a website that properly represented me. I did have focus, determination and divine support when I committed to my first multi-authored book collaboration. Even with no sales the first two months of the year, I am on track to have my first six-figure year and will be scaling to multiple six figures for 2022.

I have always loved books, reading, writing and helping people and now I get to combine all of these! This work has pushed me to levels of myself and as a leader incredibly quickly. I went from unpredictable income and client loads to 5 figure months within weeks, hired more support staff, and have a level of fulfillment that is ever growing. It's like I finally found the right path on the map of life and am happily planning out future events, projects and aspects, all while creating my own hours and spending time with my family.

ABOUT JESSICA

Jessica Verrill is the founder of House of Indigo, a publishing house focused on the growth of heart-centered and spiritual leaders.

Her skills as an intuitive coach and energetic alchemist supports high levels of growth and alignment, while working directly as a channel to her personal guides. As a life-long learner, she is often immersed in books and classes, including all aspects of herbalism and flower essences, health, wellness and personal development, spirituality, and enhanced psychic development.

Jessica lives in Maine with her husband, daughter, and black lab. She loves gardening, communing with nature spirits, hiking, exploring nature, being around water, and traveling.

For information on publishing opportunities, courses and more visit: *www.house-indigo.com*

SHANNON VAN DEN BERG

I'm Shannon Van Den Berg and I founded Kiva Publishing in February 2021. I was an online feminine leadership mentor for eight years before starting my publishing company. I helped moms step into the bigness of their soul purpose so they could call in higher levels of impact and income and activate their divine feminine leadership role. My work was a synergy of intuitive self-healing, embodiment practices, mindset work and channeled activations. Before going online, I created a local healing center, ran a successful shamanic sound healing practice, and channeled my inner medicine woman through my herbal store filled with crystals, books and plant medicine remedies—all while going to midwifery school, having three boys under 3 years old and growing a construction company with my husband.

After being part of my first bestselling multi-author book, I was hooked. I'd dreamed of becoming an author since I was 4 years old. I'd been published in magazines numerous times since I was a teenager, but getting published in a book had been unreachable until I was asked into that first multi-author book. I waited almost 20 years for that opportunity!

I joined two more multi-author books right away and planned to be part of six multi-author books in 2021. Then I realized I could elevate the feminine leaders I work with by starting my own publishing house. I'd fallen totally in love with the model Adriana created. The genuine collaboration; the beautiful synergy of women supporting each other and working together to create a massive ripple of transformation in the world; the deep connection created through a story that has people showing up ready to buy; and the initiation and growth you go through as you fully express yourself and your soul mission. All of it.

As I announced founding my publishing company and began filling spots, I realized I needed to go beyond my cozy loyal community that had been with me for years. I started using lead generation posts and connecting with potential authors in Facebook groups—exactly what Adriana teaches. It started working; slowly at first, and then faster. I learned how to communicate better via messenger and then started sharing the opportunity with coaches who shared it with their communities. Authors invited in new authors and I started having multiple authors join a day. It was really exciting to see the model actually work the way it was presented.

Starting my own publishing company has allowed me to embody a total quantum leap in my life and business. I had my first five-figure month ever. I found all my prior skills and experience translated into value and resources for my authors. I'm able to take my authors to meet the ancient storytellers that guide them, learn how to intuitively channel their stories, heal and release as they move through the journey, and support and guide them as they write.

I learned to do things my way and actually gave myself permission to be more of who I am online. I gave up long held fears about how my success would take me away from being a good mom and change the dynamics with my husband when I started making more money than we do in our construction business. I learned that being excited about what you do makes you even more present for your kids and creates a deeply fulfilled mom who models changing the world. It helped me step into the CEO role of my business being able to do business with ease, fun, flow and creativity. I'm able to focus on the relationships and impacts that are reasons I started my business.

ABOUT SHANNON

Shannon Van Den Berg is a three-time international bestselling author, Feminine Leadership mentor, and the CEO and founder of Kiva Publishing. She provides a platform for powerful women leaders to share their story and message so they can have a massive impact in the world.

Shannon specializes in guiding her clients to activate their inner Creatrix and Divine Storyteller so they can cultivate an epic life and unlock deeper levels of service, impact and wealth in their business.

She lives on her ranch in the sacred Four Corners area of Hesperus, Colorado with her husband and four homeschooled boys.

Shannon has made nearly $20k in her first two months of owning her own publishing house. You can find her at *www.shannonvandenberg.com/kivapublishing* where she quantum leaps female business owners into fully expressed, highly visible bestselling authors.

Are you ready to become our next success story? Let us know in the Facebook Group. Sign up for my free masterclass to get access to the group:

www.adrianamoniquealvarez.com/how-to-start-your-own-publishing-company

9

Energetically Connect To Your Clients

*T*he way you arrived here, with this book in your hands, is partially due to the energetic work I do daily and partially due to the desires in your own heart.

We meet here and it is no accident.

I tend to attract many women who are spiritual and who are aware of their connection to Source, God —whatever you call it.

In this book, I was asked to share this process I use in every aspect of my business. I usually leave this unspoken until after someone becomes a client. I can no longer keep business to the left and spirit to the right when I show up in the world. It is time to bring it all together. Integrate and unify.

The 10,000 women who are going to start their

publishing company with us by 2027 are feeling the same way.

It is time to be completely comfortable receiving large amounts of money, being disciplined, consistent, and business savvy.

To also be deeply connected with our soul's work, our mission, who we are here to create with. Deliberately being guided and supported by our Angels, Guides, and Ancestors.

We do not need any more broke change makers.

And we do not need any more soulless success.

We are ushering in a movement that celebrates women who are integrated, whole, thriving in every way, unapologetic, and Divine.

The way I connect energetically to my clients is by creating a designated place, often on posterboard, where I write the name of the book, program, or project at the top.

Then I create a space for each person on that page. This can be through hearts, lines, or circles.

At the bottom I write, I call in my soul-aligned dream clients from the north, south, east, and west. May they have the courage to say yes to themselves and the resources to say yes to me. So it is!

Each day I sit with this paper, sending love and courage to each person who will end up being on the project. I tell them I have prepared a place for them. I share with them my commitment to showing up, using my voice, my words, so they can find me easily.

I ask our unseen team to create synchronicities. To bring us closer each day. To put my books, videos, and voice on the top of their feed, in their hands, right in front of them.

I feel them and see us moving together.

Then I say, I am choosing to be the most consistent person I know.

I choose to wake up every day and say, "I know there are women who are asking for what I have."

I choose to be consistently optimistic.

I choose to be consistently present.

I choose to be consistently inviting.

I choose to be consistently showing up.

I choose to be consistently praying.

I choose to be consistently calling women in to their soul's work.

I do this so when I get to the end of my days, I can say I wholeheartedly lived this life, and there are signs that this is true.

LEAVE THE WORLD TANGIBLE SIGNS THAT YOU WALKED HERE.

It's your time!

10

Don't Wait - Start Now!

*G*etting started is the hardest part. Once you are in our dynamic community, once you are rubbing shoulders with women who are doing big things, you have more courage than you ever have.

Every day I ask my Angels, Guides, and Ancestors to gather the women who are meant to be here. I do not have any desire to anyone outside of that. We will not chase you down, or put you under a high pressure spell.

Your heart is probably beating a little faster.

You are hearing yes and now it is completely up to you to choose it. We have success stories being made every day. The model works and the world is waiting.

If you are ready to step up, we have three ways we can work together.

As soon as you opt-in to watch the Masterclass you will see these three options and if you have questions or need someone to chat with, this is available.

We have a leadership team that is here to support you from spiritual to practical business to leadership to launches. You have everything you need to succeed and fast.

We would love to have you join the revolution.

www.adrianamoniquealvarez.com/how-to-start-your-own-publishing-company

FAQ

1. How do I start a publishing company?

There are several ways you can get started, but what I have developed is the most profitable way to get started. Publishing companies can be like any creative endeavor, heavy on creativity and light on cash flow.

I do not buy into that model or mindset.

I teach my clients how to start with one multi-author book and expand into solo books, company books, and high-end offers that fit them like a glove.

2. What is the process of working with authors?

Successfully working with authors means you have a clear framework to support them in their journey.

I have created a process — and timelines — that gets books released months, if not years faster than traditional publishers.

I teach my clients how to walk authors through this as well as how to hire a team that supports them so they are not editing and formatting books.

3. How do I release quality work?

It starts with working with high-quality clients. Positioning and marketing are key in ensuring you are working with the best authors. In addition to this, I teach my clients how to hire a team of experts in their respective fields. Each component of the books is first class.

4. How do I start and integrate with my current business?

I added publishing to my already established business and have helped my clients do the same. The best answer is it depends. My job is to look at what you have going on in your business and offer a couple of strategies that will best fit you and your goals.

5. What if I don't have any experience?

Everyone has experience in something. The important thing is to assess what you have done and how you can best leverage your experiences to launch your publishing company. Give yourself credit and don't be afraid to get loud and proud about what you are good at.

6. How do I generate the money to get started?

I'm so glad you asked. What I know is every time I have wanted something, I figured it out. The truth is, if you let your desire inspire you, you will figure it out in record time. You will wake up with an idea and boom it will be done. Many of my clients also go through the steps in this book and get a handful of Yes's and use that to get started. The truth is this is a necessary imitation because the entire process will require you to get creative and resourceful, might as well start now.

7. How do I choose the best topics?

Start by asking, what are the best topics for ME? There are not best topics, simply the ones you want to talk about and gather stories about. Don't overthink; go with your gut and the suggestions I've offered in this book.

8. What if technology is not my strong suit?

If technology isn't your strong suit and you want to start a business online, having a team is non-negotiable. I like to stay in my zone of genius and hire everything else out. This means you need to factor in what it would cost you to have a personal assistant and tech support into what you charge.

9. How do I handle the legal aspects?

In the AMA Certification Program, we help our clients create terms and conditions that cover their tush and create clear boundaries of what is included and what is not.

10. Are kids' books a good option?

Short answer, no. I highly recommend focusing on non-fiction books for professionals for at least your first year in publishing and then you can decide if you would like to expand.

11. How do you market the books so they hit bestseller status on Amazon?

Oh, the secret sauce is what we teach in the AMA Certification 1.0 Program. We have many strategies so you can guarantee that your book will hit the best-seller lists.

12. Is it a profitable business model?

Yes! Owning a publishing house is one of the most profitable and in-demand businesses I know of right now and I am always looking for what's hot.

13. What if I just started another business?

If you just started another business I would look at how you can incorporate and weave the two if possible. For example, can your other business become an up-sell in a publishing business or is it completely separate? If you are still creating clients and traction in another business, it comes down to what you have to invest. If you can hire an appointment setter or salesperson in addition to the rest of your team it could work, if not, I recommend waiting until you have either stability in your other business or capital to invest in publishing.

14. How long does it take to get into cash flow?

It depends. I have some clients that make $8k in their first week and others that take two months to get a client. It really depends on how much time, energy, and focus you have to put into your new publishing company and whether or not you have an audience or a network you can tap into. Attitude and determination are what ultimately determine how quickly things start flowing. If it is obvious that you are a woman on a mission, other people will jump on your project.

15. How many books can I do a year?

That is completely up to you and what you want to create. While we offer guidance for our clients, we do not set any limits on what they can do. There are truly no limits!

16. What is the timeframe to produce a book?

It typically takes 3 months to produce a book once it is sold out.

17. How can I scale this business?

Once again there are so many ways. In the AMA 2.0 Certification, I teach women how to make $30k a month and scale to $80k+ months. This happens in a variety of ways but the two most important ingredients are the desire to do and the ability to see it as possible for you.

18. Do you provide solid assistance in the certification program?

Absolutely! If you choose the Home Study option, you have access to a comprehensive training library as well as invitations to our monthly intensives at a discounted rate.

If you choose the group program, you are part of a vibrant group where you can ask questions between the weekly training calls.

If you choose the private 1:1 option, you will have weekly calls and Voxer support between calls.

About Adriana Monique Alvarez

Adriana Monique Alvarez was never tamed by higher education, corporate culture, or status quo. From the beginning she has taken the path less traveled. Her heart took her overseas as a volunteer in her 20's. Working with children in orphanages in Myanmar, Albania, and Kenya. After contracting the deadliest strain of malaria she decided to return to the United States and only a short time later met her husband Derek and they started a business together, mainly because they were both unemployable.

Together they have built a life they love which included traveling to Albania, Greece, and Montenegro together. They continued their travels after having two sons. Taking their sons to see Mexico from top to bottom, every treasure in all of Italy and Eastern Europe while growing the business.

They now reside in the middle of nowhere Colorado where they are learning how to change the world of publishing while also learning how to homestead, raise chickens, start a greenhouse, homeschool, and camp on the weekends.

Adriana is a number one international bestselling author, Wall Street Journal bestselling author, and has been featured in Forbes yada yada. What matters is she knows how to light a fire and extract the highest and best from every woman who comes near her. Her spirit animal is the honey badger and once she sinks her teeth into something, there is no turning back.

You can learn more about the work she does and the amazing clients she serves at:

www.AdrianaMoniqueAlvarez.com

Made in the USA
Middletown, DE
25 October 2022